Innovate or Stagnate
A Guide to Entrepreneurial Success

Introduction:

Importance of Innovation in Entrepreneurship:

Innovation is the cornerstone of entrepreneurial success for several key reasons:

1. Competitive Edge: Innovation allows businesses to differentiate themselves in crowded markets, attracting customers with unique offerings and solutions.

2. Adaptation to Change: In rapidly evolving industries, innovation enables businesses to pivot and seize new opportunities, ensuring survival in changing market conditions.

3. Problem Solving: Entrepreneurs are essentially problem-solvers, and innovation is the engine that drives creative solutions to customer pain points.

4. Efficiency and Productivity: Innovations in processes and technology can boost efficiency, reduce costs, and maximize productivity, vital for resource-constrained startups.

5. Customer-Centric Approach: Innovators focus on understanding and meeting customer needs, fostering strong customer loyalty and brand recognition.

6. Sustainability: Innovation is key to building a business that can thrive long-term by adapting to market shifts and challenges.

7. Talent Attraction: Innovative companies often attract top talent, drawing individuals seeking opportunities for creativity and growth.

8. Market Expansion: Innovation opens doors to new markets and customer segments, enabling entrepreneurs to scale their businesses.

9. Inspiration and Vision: Innovation fuels ambitious visions and encourages entrepreneurs to aim high, driving success.

10. Global Impact: Innovation has the potential to transform industries, shape societies, and change the world, making it a powerful force in entrepreneurship.

Why Stagnation Can Be the Death Knell of a Business:

Stagnation can be disastrous for businesses due to several reasons:

1. Loss of Relevance: In fast-paced markets, stagnant businesses quickly lose relevance as they fail to keep up with evolving customer needs and industry trends.

2. Competitive Erosion: Stagnant businesses lose their competitive edge, allowing more innovative competitors to capture market share.

3. Declining Morale: Stagnation often leads to employee dissatisfaction and disengagement, impacting productivity and overall company culture.

4. Missed Opportunities: Failing to innovate means missing out on new revenue streams and emerging markets.

5. Risk of Disruption: Stagnant businesses are vulnerable to disruptive forces, such as new technologies or market entrants, which can quickly render their offerings obsolete.

6. Profit Erosion: Without innovation, cost-efficiency and profitability suffer, putting financial sustainability at risk.

7. Loss of Customers: Customers seek better, more innovative solutions. Stagnant businesses risk losing their customer base to competitors.

8. Inability to Adapt: Stagnation can lead to an inability to adapt to unforeseen challenges and changes in the business environment

The Roadmap to Entrepreneurial Success:

A roadmap to entrepreneurial success typically includes the following key steps:

1. Idea Generation Start by generating innovative business ideas that address a specific market need or problem.

2. Market Research: Conduct thorough market research to validate your ideas and understand your target audience.

3. Business Plan: Develop a comprehensive business plan that outlines your vision, goals, strategies, and financial projections.

4. Funding and Resources: Secure the necessary funding and resources to launch and sustain your business.

5. Product/Service Development: Create your products or services, focusing on quality, uniqueness, and customer value.

6. Marketing and Branding: Develop a marketing strategy to promote your offerings and build a strong brand identity.

7. Customer Acquisition: Attract your first customers and continually grow your customer base.

8. Operational Excellence: Establish efficient processes and ensure effective management of resources.

9. Adaptation and Innovation: Continuously adapt to market changes, innovate to stay competitive, and plan for long-term sustainability.

10. Scaling and Growth: Once established, focus on scaling your business and expanding into new markets.

11. Monitoring and Evaluation: Regularly monitor performance, gather feedback, and evaluate your strategies to make necessary adjustments.

12. Resilience and Persistence: Entrepreneurial success often requires resilience and persistence in the face of challenges and setbacks.

Remember, success in entrepreneurship is a dynamic process that often involves iteration and learning from both successes and failures.

Chapter one

Innovation mindset:

Embracing a Culture of Innovation:

Fostering Creativity: An innovation mindset encourages a workplace environment where creativity is nurtured. It means giving employees the freedom to brainstorm, experiment, and think outside the box.

Open Communication: In an innovative culture, open communication is vital. Ideas flow freely, and individuals feel comfortable sharing their thoughts and suggestions without fear of criticism.

Risk Tolerance: Innovation often involves taking calculated risks. In an innovative culture, there's an acceptance of failure as a part of the learning process, and a willingness to take risks to explore new possibilities.

Continuous Learning: The culture promotes continuous learning and adaptation. It recognizes that innovation is an ongoing process, and employees are encouraged to stay updated and adapt to changing circumstances.

Collaboration: Innovation thrives in a collaborative environment. People from different backgrounds and departments work together to solve problems and create new solutions.

The Power of Creative Thinking:

Divergent Thinking: Creative thinking is about divergent thinking, which means generating a multitude of ideas and exploring various possibilities without premature judgment.

Unconventional Solutions: Creative thinking often leads to unconventional solutions that can disrupt the status quo and bring about positive change.

Problem-Solving: Creative thinking is a valuable problem-solving tool. It helps individuals approach challenges from different angles and find innovative ways to address them.

Visualization: Creative thinkers often visualize their ideas, seeing the big picture and understanding how different elements fit together to create a cohesive whole.

Inspiration: Creative thinking can be a source of inspiration, motivating individuals to explore new concepts, experiment, and push boundaries.

Overcoming the Fear of Failure:

Learning Opportunity: An innovation mindset reframes failure as a learning opportunity. It acknowledges that some of the most significant breakthroughs come after initial failures.

Resilience: It encourages individuals to be resilient and not be discouraged by setbacks. A fear of failure can stifle creativity, while resilience allows people to keep trying and learning from their mistakes.

Iterative Process: An innovation mindset recognizes that success often involves iterating, refining, and improving ideas over time. This approach reduces the fear of initial failure.

Risk Management: It doesn't advocate reckless risk-taking but rather calculated risks. It means assessing the potential risks and rewards of an idea and proceeding thoughtfully.

Supportive Environment: A culture that encourages innovation should also provide support and guidance for those who face the fear of failure, helping them navigate challenges and grow from their experiences.

Embracing an innovation mindset, fostering creative thinking, and overcoming the fear of failure are essential components for individuals and organizations looking to drive innovation and stay competitive in today's fast-paced world.

Chapter Two

Identifying opportunity

Recognizing Market Gaps and Needs:

Observation and Empathy: Identifying opportunities begins with keen observation and empathy. Entrepreneurs should pay close attention to daily life, interact with potential customers, and understand their pain points and unmet needs.

Gap Analysis: Conduct a gap analysis by assessing what is currently available in the market and comparing it to what customers truly desire. Identifying the disparities between existing solutions and customer expectations is the foundation for innovation.

Innovative Solutions: Recognizing market gaps and needs presents an opportunity to develop innovative solutions that directly address specific problems or unfulfilled demands.

Analyzing Trends and Emerging Technologies:

Stay Informed: Entrepreneurs should stay informed about industry trends and emerging technologies through continuous learning and monitoring industry publications, blogs, and attending relevant conferences and events.

Technology Adoption Understanding the potential impact of emerging technologies is crucial. Entrepreneurs must evaluate how new technologies can be applied to their industry or business to gain a competitive advantage.

Disruption Analysis: Analyzing trends and emerging technologies also involves identifying potential disruptive forces that could reshape the market landscape, providing entrepreneurs with opportunities for innovation and adaptation.

Conducting Market Research:

Customer Insights: Market research involves gathering insights about customer preferences, behaviors, and demographics. It helps in creating customer personas and tailoring products or services to specific target audiences.

Competitor Analysis: Understanding the competitive landscape is essential. Analyzing competitors' strengths and weaknesses can reveal opportunities to differentiate and outperform them.

Market Sizing: Entrepreneurs need to assess the size of the market they intend to enter. This information guides decisions about market entry, pricing, and scaling.

Validation: Market research validates the demand for a product or service. It helps ensure that there is a viable market for the entrepreneurial idea, reducing the risk of launching something with limited appeal.

-Feedback Loop: Continuous market research establishes a feedback loop with customers. Gathering and acting upon customer feedback enables businesses to adapt to changing market conditions and evolving customer needs.

Risk Mitigation: Market research can help identify potential risks and challenges, allowing entrepreneurs to develop strategies to mitigate these risks and increase the chances of success.

Identifying opportunities through recognizing market gaps and needs, analyzing trends and emerging technologies, and conducting comprehensive market research is a foundational step in the entrepreneurial journey. It provides the necessary insights to develop solutions that resonate with customers and can lead to entrepreneurial success.

Chapter Three

Nurturing Creativity:

Encouraging Idea Generation:

Open Dialogue: Promote an environment where open dialogue and brainstorming are encouraged. Make employees or team members feel comfortable sharing their ideas, no matter how unconventional they may seem.

Diverse Perspectives: Embrace diverse perspectives and backgrounds within your team. Different viewpoints can lead to more innovative ideas and solutions.

Inspiration from Outside: Encourage individuals to draw inspiration from outside their usual scope. Attend conferences, read widely, and explore different industries to gain fresh insights.

Problem-Solving Sessions: Organize problem-solving sessions where team members collaboratively tackle challenges and generate ideas collectively. Recognition and Rewards: Recognize and reward innovative thinking to motivate employees to continue generating new ideas.

Fostering a Creative Workspace:

Physical Environment: Design a physical workspace that is conducive to creativity. Incorporate elements like comfortable seating, natural light, and flexible work areas.

Minimal Distractions: Minimize distractions and interruptions in the workspace to allow individuals to focus on creative tasks.

Inspiring Decor: Decorate the workspace with art, inspirational quotes, and elements that stimulate creative thinking.

Collaborative Spaces: Create areas where team members can collaborate and brainstorm, fostering a sense of community and idea exchange.

Innovation Tools: Provide tools and resources that support creativity, such as whiteboards, brainstorming software, and access to a variety of materials.

Techniques for Boosting Creativity:

Mind Mapping: Use mind mapping techniques to visually organize thoughts and ideas, facilitating the exploration of interconnected concepts.

Reverse Brainstorming: Instead of generating ideas, focus on identifying problems or challenges. Then, brainstorm solutions by reversing the typical thought process.

- Divergent Thinking: Encourage divergent thinking by exploring as many ideas as possible without judgment or constraint.

Storytelling: Storytelling can stimulate creative thinking. Encourage team members to create narratives around ideas, envisioning how they would play out in real-life scenarios.

Cross-Disciplinary Learning: Promote learning across various disciplines to expose individuals to new perspectives and methodologies.

Brain Breaks: Incorporate regular breaks to refresh and rejuvenate the mind. Short walks, meditation, or creative exercises can help clear mental blocks and boost creativity.

Experimentation: Encourage a culture of experimentation and innovation, where taking risks and learning from failures is valued.

Nurturing creativity is essential for generating innovative ideas and solutions. By encouraging idea generation, creating a creative workspace, and implementing techniques to boost creativity, organizations can foster an environment where innovation thrives and leads to positive outcomes.

Chapter Four

Developingg innovative products and services

let's explore the process of developing innovative products and services, including the stages from concept to prototype, testing and refining the innovation, and the critical balance between risk and reward:

From Concept to Prototype

Conceptualization: The journey of developing innovative products and services begins with a clear and compelling concept. This concept should address a specific problem or opportunity, providing a unique and valuable solution.

Design and Planning: Following the initial concept, meticulous design and planning are essential. This stage involves creating detailed specifications, blueprints, and a roadmap for transforming the concept into a tangible prototype.

Prototyping: The creation of a prototype is a pivotal step in the development process. A prototype is a preliminary, working model of the product or service, serving as a proof of concept. It allows you to visualize the idea, test its feasibility, and make necessary adjustments.

Iterative Refinement: Prototyping often involves multiple iterations and refinements. Feedback from users, experts, or stakeholders is invaluable for fine-tuning the innovation, ensuring it aligns with user expectations and market demands.

Testing and Refining Your Innovation:

Market Testing: After the prototype is ready, it's crucial to test it in the real market environment. Collect feedback from potential customers and stakeholders to gauge their reactions, needs, and preferences.

Feedback Integration: Use the feedback obtained during market testing to improve the prototype. This phase involves design enhancements, feature additions or modifications, and any necessary changes to better align the innovation with the target audience's expectations.

Usability Assessment: Evaluate the innovation's usability by conducting user testing. This phase helps identify any user experience issues or bottlenecks, ensuring that the product or service is user-friendly.

Scalability and Efficiency: Assess the scalability and efficiency of your innovation. Consider whether it can be produced or delivered efficiently and cost-effectively, especially as the product or service gains traction and user numbers grow.

Beta Testing: Conduct beta testing by releasing the innovation to a limited group of users for further in-depth feedback. Beta testers can help uncover potential technical issues or performance problems.

Balancing Risk and Reward

Risk Assessment: Thoroughly assess potential risks associated with the innovation. These risks may include market competition, technological challenges, financial constraints, or regulatory hurdles.

Cost-Benefit Analysis: Perform a cost-benefit analysis to weigh potential rewards against the risks and investments. Determine whether the innovation has the potential to generate significant value and whether the investment is justifiable.

Risk Mitigation: Develop risk mitigation strategies. These strategies can encompass contingency plans, securing additional funding sources, and addressing legal and regulatory compliance.

Milestone-Based Approach:Implement a milestone-based approach to the development process. This means evaluating progress and results at key stages. Decisions on whether to proceed, pivot, or adjust are made based on the outcomes at each milestone.

Flexibility and Adaptability: Be prepared to adapt as circumstances evolve. The ability to pivot and make strategic adjustments is essential for maintaining the balance between risk and reward.

Long-Term Vision: Consider the long-term vision for the innovation. While immediate risks may exist, the potential for sustained rewards over time can justify calculated risks and investments.

Balancing risk and reward is a fundamental aspect of innovation. Successful development of innovative products and services involves a structured approach that moves from concept to prototype, incorporates thorough testing and refinement, and carefully considers the risks and potential rewards associated with the endeavor. This dynamic process responds to evolving conditions and feedback, ultimately aiming to bring valuable and groundbreaking innovations to the market.

Chapter Five

Building Dynamic Team

Certainly, here are notes on building a dynamic team, which involves recruiting innovative talent, promoting collaboration through cross-functional teams, and fostering effective leadership in an innovative environment:

Recruiting Innovative Talent

Recognizing Innovation in Candidates: When recruiting for an innovative team, it's essential to identify candidates with a track record of innovation, creative problem-solving, and the ability to think outside the box. Look for examples of their past contributions to innovative projects.

Diverse Skill Sets: An innovative team should consist of individuals with diverse skill sets, backgrounds, and experiences. Diversity can lead to a wide range of perspectives and ideas, which is essential for innovation.

Cultural Fit: Beyond skills, assess candidates for their cultural fit with the organization's innovation goals. They should share the company's values and be excited about the opportunity to contribute to innovation.

Fostering a Culture of Innovation: Ensure that your organization fosters a culture of innovation from the outset. Prospective candidates should be aware of the company's commitment to innovation, making it an attractive place for innovative individuals to work.

Collaboration and Cross-Functional Teams:

Cross-Functional Teams: Encourage cross-functional teams by bringing together individuals from different departments or areas of expertise. This diversity of knowledge and skills can lead to innovative problem-solving and product development.

Clear Communication: Effective collaboration relies on clear and open communication. Team members should be encouraged to share their ideas, ask questions, and provide feedback freely.

Shared Goals: Ensure that cross-functional teams have clear, shared goals. This helps keep everyone aligned and working toward common objectives.

Regular Meetings and Updates: Schedule regular meetings and updates to keep team members informed about progress, challenges, and opportunities. This helps maintain momentum and focus.

Conflict Resolution: Conflicts may arise in cross-functional teams due to differing perspectives. Establish effective conflict resolution processes to address and resolve disagreements constructively.

Leadership in an Innovative Environment:

Lead by Example: Leaders should exemplify innovative thinking and demonstrate a commitment to fostering a culture of innovation. Their behavior sets the tone for the entire team.

Empowerment: Empower team members to take ownership of their projects and contribute to the innovation process. Encourage autonomy and self-directed decision-making within a framework of shared goals.

Risk Tolerance: Leadership in an innovative environment requires a degree of risk tolerance. Leaders should be willing to support calculated risks and not penalize failures as long as they lead to learning and growth.

Recognition and Rewards: Implement a system for recognizing and rewarding innovative contributions. This can include monetary incentives, promotions, or public acknowledgment of exceptional work.

Adaptability: In an innovative environment, leadership must be adaptable and responsive to changing circumstances. Leaders should be able to pivot and adjust strategies based on evolving market conditions or insights.

Building a dynamic team in an innovative environment involves recruiting talent with innovative capabilities, promoting effective collaboration through cross-functional teams, and providing leadership that fosters a culture of innovation. A well-structured and innovative team can drive forward-thinking solutions and contribute to the organization's overall success.

Chapter Six

Adapting to Change

Adopting to change, include ivoting in response to market shifts, managing

uncertainty, and staying agile and resilient:

Pivoting in Response to Market Shifts:

Market Sensitivity: Pivoting is the ability to sense changes in the market and

quickly adjust strategies and offerings. It involves being attuned to shifts in

customer needs, preferences, or emerging trends.

Adaptability: A business that pivots effectively can adapt its products, services,

or business model to better align with the evolving market landscape. This

adaptability allows the business to seize new opportunities and overcome

challenges.

Customer-Centric Approach: A successful pivot often revolves around

understanding and catering to the changing needs and desires of customers. This

means actively seeking customer feedback and using it to inform pivoting

decisions.

Data-Driven Decision-Making: Pivoting decisions should be data-driven. Analyzing market data, customer behavior, and industry trends can provide valuable insights for making informed changes.

Managing Uncertainty:

Risk Assessment: In uncertain times, it's crucial to conduct thorough risk assessments. Identify potential risks, evaluate their impact, and develop contingency plans to mitigate them.

Scenario Planning: Scenario planning involves creating a range of plausible scenarios for the future. By envisioning different outcomes, businesses can prepare for various possibilities, reducing the impact of uncertainty.

Financial Prudence: In uncertain times, maintaining a strong financial position is vital. Businesses should manage cash flow carefully, cut unnecessary expenses, and secure additional sources of funding when needed.

Agile Decision-Making: Being agile in decision-making is key to managing uncertainty. Businesses should be ready to pivot quickly when necessary and not hesitate in taking action when faced with ambiguity.

Staying Agile and Resilient:

Agility: Business agility refers to the ability to respond rapidly to change. Agile businesses often have streamlined processes, empowered employees, and a culture of experimentation.

Innovation: Staying agile and resilient requires continuous innovation. Encourage employees to generate creative solutions, adapt to new circumstances, and explore novel approaches to problems.

Resilience: Resilience is the capacity to bounce back from adversity. Resilient businesses have a crisis management plan in place and can recover from setbacks or disruptions effectively.

Learning Orientation: A culture of learning and adaptation is essential for staying agile and resilient. Businesses should encourage ongoing learning and development among their teams.

Leadership: Effective leadership plays a crucial role in fostering agility and resilience. Leaders should set the tone, communicate a clear vision, and provide support during times of change.

Adopting to change, including pivoting in response to market shifts, managing uncertainty, and staying agile and resilient, is critical in today's dynamic business environment. Businesses that can effectively navigate change are better positioned to not only survive but also thrive in the face of uncertainty and disruption.

Chapter Seven

Marketing and Branding

Marketing and rebranding innovation, focusing on storytelling and positioning, communicating your unique value proposition, and leveraging digital marketing for innovation:

Storytelling and Positioning:

Crafting a Compelling Narrative: Storytelling is a powerful tool for conveying your brand's innovation. Create a compelling narrative that explains the journey and purpose behind your innovation. This narrative should resonate with your audience and connect emotionally.

Building a Strong Brand Identity: Your brand's identity should align with your innovation. It's not just about what you offer but also how you present it. Ensure that your brand's messaging, visuals, and overall tone reflect the innovative spirit of your product or service.

Defining Your Position in the Market: Clearly define your position in the market. Explain how your innovation is different from existing solutions and how it addresses specific customer needs or pain points. Position your brand as a pioneer in the industry.

Consistency in Messaging: Maintain consistency in your messaging across all marketing channels. Whether it's your website, social media, or advertising, the messaging should reinforce your innovation story and position.

Communicating Your Unique Value Proposition:

Defining Your Value Proposition: Clearly articulate your unique value proposition (UVP). What sets your innovation apart? How does it solve a problem or improve the lives of your customers? Your UVP should be succinct and easy to understand.

Customer-Centric Approach: Focus on the benefits your innovation brings to the customer. Address the "what's in it for me" question that potential customers may have. Explain how your product or service can enhance their lives or meet their needs.

Demonstrating Real-World Impact: Use case studies, testimonials, and real-world examples to showcase the impact of your innovation. Provide evidence of its effectiveness in solving problems or creating value for customers.

Highlighting Competitive Advantages: Emphasize any competitive advantages you have over existing solutions. Whether it's price, quality, speed, or some other aspect, make sure customers are aware of what makes your innovation superior.

Leveraging Digital Marketing for Innovation:

Content Marketing: Utilize content marketing to educate and inform your audience about your innovation. Create blogs, articles, videos, and infographics that explain its features, benefits, and use cases.

Social Media Engagement: Engage with your audience on social media platforms. Share updates about your innovation, respond to questions and comments, and create conversations around its value.

Email Marketing: Use email marketing to nurture leads and keep your audience informed about your innovation's progress. Email campaigns can also highlight special offers or incentives.

Online Advertising: Consider paid online advertising channels like Google Ads and social media ads to reach a broader audience. Target your ads to reach those who are most likely to be interested in your innovation.

Data Analytics: Leverage data analytics to track the performance of your digital marketing efforts. Analyze user behavior, conversion rates, and other metrics to fine-tune your strategies for better results.

Incorporating storytelling and positioning, communicating your unique value proposition, and leveraging digital marketing are integral to successfully marketing and rebranding innovation. These strategies not only promote your innovation but also engage and educate your target audience, building excitement and anticipation for your innovative product or service.

Chapter Eight

Scaling and Growth

Scaling and growth, covers strategies for sustainable growth, expanding into new markets, and the importance of balancing scale and innovation:

Strategies for Sustainable Growth:

Customer-Centric Approach: A customer-centric strategy focuses on delivering exceptional value to existing customers and retaining their loyalty. It often involves offering additional products or services that meet their evolving needs.

Product Diversification: Expanding your product or service offerings to cater to a broader range of customer needs. This can involve launching complementary products or targeting new customer segments.

Market Penetration: Deepening your market penetration in existing regions by gaining more customers or increasing the frequency of their purchases. This can be achieved through marketing, advertising, or sales strategies.

Operational Efficiency: Implementing process improvements and cost-saving measures to optimize operations. This can free up resources to invest in growth initiatives.

Partnerships and Alliances: Collaborating with strategic partners, such as other businesses or industry players, can provide access to new customers, technologies, or distribution channels, fostering growth.

Expanding into New Markets:

Market Research: Thoroughly research potential new markets to understand their dynamics, customer preferences, and competition. Assess the feasibility and readiness for expansion.

Localization: Tailor your products, services, and marketing to suit the specific needs and cultural nuances of the new market. Localization enhances your relevance and appeal.

Entry Strategies: Determine the entry strategy, whether it's through mergers and acquisitions, partnerships, franchising, or starting from scratch. The choice should align with your business goals and available resources.

Regulatory Compliance: Understand the legal and regulatory requirements of the new market. Ensure compliance to avoid setbacks or legal issues.

Risk Mitigation: Develop a comprehensive risk mitigation plan, accounting for factors such as currency fluctuations, political instability, and market volatility in the new territory.

Balancing Scale and Innovation:

Innovation Culture: Cultivate a culture of innovation even as your business scales. Encourage employees at all levels to contribute fresh ideas, experiment, and take calculated risks.

Incremental vs. Disruptive Innovation: Balance incremental innovations that optimize existing processes with disruptive innovations that have the potential to revolutionize your industry.

Resource Allocation: Allocate resources to support both ongoing operations and innovation initiatives. This might involve setting aside budgets, dedicated teams, or innovation labs.

Feedback Loops: Maintain feedback loops to assess the impact of innovations on your scaling efforts. Gather input from customers, employees, and stakeholders to ensure that innovations align with growth objectives.

Agility: Maintain agility in your operations, allowing you to adapt to changing market conditions and emerging opportunities. Agility is key to scaling efficiently while fostering innovation.

Scaling and growth are crucial steps in an organization's journey. Implementing sustainable growth strategies, expanding into new markets, and finding the right balance between scale and innovation are essential for achieving long-term success. These efforts should be underpinned by a clear vision and a commitment to delivering value to customers

Chapter Nine

Case Studies in Entrepreneurial and innovation

Case studies in entrepreneurial innovation, showcasing real-world examples of innovating entrepreneurs and exploring the valuable lessons we can derive from their successes and failures:

Real-World Examples of Innovating Entrepreneurs:

Steve Jobs and Apple: Steve Jobs, the co-founder of Apple Inc., is known for his innovative approach to product design and user experience. The introduction of game-changing devices like the iPhone and iPad revolutionized entire industries.

Elon Musk and SpaceX: Elon Musk's SpaceX has transformed the aerospace industry with innovations in reusable rocket technology. This has significantly reduced the cost of space exploration and redefined space travel.

Jeff Bezos and Amazon: Jeff Bezos founded Amazon, which began as an online bookstore but evolved into an e-commerce giant. Amazon's innovative approaches include Prime shipping, Kindle e-readers, and AWS (Amazon Web Services).

Mark Zuckerberg and Facebook: Mark Zuckerberg's creation of Facebook, and later acquisitions like Instagram and WhatsApp, reshaped social media and how people connect globally.

Sara Blakely and Spanx: Sara Blakely's Spanx disrupted the fashion industry with innovative undergarments that offered a sleek look. She turned an idea into a billion-dollar business.

Reed Hastings and Netflix: Reed Hastings founded Netflix, which revolutionized the entertainment industry by introducing streaming services and original content production.

Brian Chesky, Joe Gebbia, and Nathan Blecharczyk and Airbnb: The founders of Airbnb transformed the hospitality sector by creating a platform for people to rent accommodations from individuals, adding a unique twist to the sharing economy.

What We Can Learn from Their Successes and Failures:

Innovative Thinking: Successful entrepreneurs exhibit innovative thinking, challenging the status quo, and identifying new opportunities. They are not afraid to disrupt traditional models.

Customer-Centric Approach: Innovating entrepreneurs often focus on understanding and serving customer needs. They prioritize user experience and satisfaction, which can drive loyalty and growth.

Risk-Taking: Entrepreneurship involves risk, and successful innovators are willing to take calculated risks. They recognize that failure is a potential outcome but view it as a valuable learning experience.

Adaptability: Entrepreneurial success is often marked by adaptability. Innovators can pivot when necessary and adjust their strategies based on changing market conditions.

Resilience: The journey of innovation can be challenging. Successful entrepreneurs are resilient and persistent, willing to persevere through failures and setbacks.

Continuous Learning: Innovating entrepreneurs are committed to continuous learning and improvement. They seek knowledge and expertise that can help them refine their ideas and execution.

Vision and Long-Term Thinking: Successful entrepreneurs have a clear vision for their innovations and often think long-term. They understand the importance of building a sustainable and impactful business.

Ethical Considerations: Innovators must consider the ethical implications of their innovations. They should ensure that their products or services benefit society and do not cause harm.

Case studies of entrepreneurial innovation provide valuable insights into the strategies, characteristics, and approaches of successful innovators. These stories of both triumphs and failures offer a wealth of knowledge for aspiring entrepreneurs and business leaders looking to make their mark in today's dynamic and evolving business landscape.

Chapter Ten

Staging Ahead in a Fast Paced World

Staying ahead in a fast-paced world, focusing on the role of lifelong learning, trends in entrepreneurship and innovation, and preparing for the future:

The Role of Lifelong Learning:

Continuous Adaptation: In a rapidly evolving world, lifelong learning is no longer an option but a necessity. It's essential for individuals and professionals to stay adaptable and relevant throughout their careers.

Skill Enhancement:Lifelong learning involves acquiring new skills and updating existing ones. It can encompass formal education, online courses, workshops, and self-directed learning.

Expanded Knowledge: Learning isn't just about skills; it's about acquiring knowledge and insights. Staying curious and informed about a wide range of topics keeps individuals well-rounded and better able to connect the dots in a dynamic world.

Critical Thinking: Lifelong learning nurtures critical thinking. It encourages individuals to question, analyze, and evaluate information, helping them make informed decisions in a rapidly changing landscape.

Innovation: Many groundbreaking innovations arise from individuals who continually seek knowledge and explore new domains. Lifelong learners are often at the forefront of innovation.

Trends in Entrepreneurship and Innovation:

Digital Transformation: The digital revolution continues to shape entrepreneurship and innovation. Businesses need to adapt to digital technologies, including AI, IoT, and blockchain, to remain competitive.

Sustainability: Sustainable and environmentally responsible practices are becoming paramount in business. Innovators are finding new ways to reduce environmental impact and cater to the growing eco-conscious market.

E-commerce and Remote Work: E-commerce and remote work trends have been accelerated, impacting traditional business models. Entrepreneurs are exploring opportunities in online retail and remote work solutions.

Health Tech: Innovations in health technology, such as telemedicine and wearable devices, are redefining healthcare delivery and wellness industries.

Collaborative Innovation: Open innovation and collaboration with partners, customers, and even competitors are emerging trends. Entrepreneurs are finding value in collective problem-solving.

Preparing for the Future:

Foresight and Strategy: Preparing for the future involves foresight and strategic planning. Businesses and individuals need to anticipate trends and challenges, setting goals to navigate what lies ahead.

Flexibility: Flexibility is crucial in adapting to the unexpected. Being willing to pivot and make strategic adjustments as circumstances change can be the key to success.

Investing in Skills: Continuous investment in skills and knowledge is a way to future-proof yourself. This involves staying current in your field and exploring adjacent areas.

Building Resilience: Building personal and professional resilience is essential. This resilience can help individuals and businesses weather storms and emerge stronger on the other side.

Sustainability: A sustainable mindset isn't just about environmental practices; it's also about the long-term viability of businesses and careers. A sustainable approach considers social, economic, and environmental factors.

In a fast-paced world, staying ahead requires a commitment to lifelong learning, an awareness of emerging trends in entrepreneurship and innovation, and a proactive approach to preparing for the future. Whether as an individual or a business, adapting to change, fostering innovation, and planning strategically are vital for not just keeping pace but leading in the dynamic landscape of today and tomorrow.

Conclusion

Conclusion, highlighting the ongoing journey of innovation and revisiting the choice between innovating and stagnating:

The Ongoing Journey of Innovation:

Innovation as a Mindset: Innovation is not a destination but a mindset. It's a way of approaching challenges, seeing opportunities, and adapting to a world that is in constant flux. The journey of innovation is unceasing, and those who embrace this mindset are better equipped to thrive in an ever-changing landscape.

Iterative and Evolving: Innovation is an iterative and evolving process. It involves cycles of ideation, experimentation, feedback, and refinement. Innovators understand that setbacks and failures are part of the journey and are viewed as valuable learning experiences.

Cultural and Organizational Shift: Organizations that foster a culture of innovation understand that it's a cultural shift. It involves empowering employees to think creatively, encouraging collaboration, and embracing risk as a necessary ingredient in the pursuit of progress.

- Staying Relevant: Staying relevant in today's fast-paced world requires a commitment to innovation. Whether in business, technology, or any field, being at the forefront demands continuous learning, adaptation, and a forward-thinking approach.

Revisiting the Choice: Innovate or Stagnate:

The Consequences of Stagnation: The consequences of stagnation are stark. In a world that is advancing at an unprecedented pace, failing to innovate can lead to obsolescence, irrelevance, and even the decline of once-thriving entities. Stagnation carries the risk of falling behind competitors and missing out on new opportunities.

The Power of Innovation: Conversely, innovation holds the power to drive progress and transform industries. Those who choose to innovate often find themselves at the vanguard of change, leading in their fields and shaping the future. Innovation opens doors to new markets, fresh solutions, and enhanced customer experiences.

Continuous Evaluation: The choice between innovating and stagnating is not a one-time decision but a continuous evaluation. It involves regularly assessing one's position, market dynamics, and the evolution of customer needs. Choosing innovation means being proactive in recognizing when change is required.

The Path Forward:As we conclude, it's clear that the path forward is one that values innovation as a guiding principle. It's a journey that celebrates the spirit of curiosity, the courage to challenge conventions, and the commitment to learning and growth. Whether as an individual, an entrepreneur, or an organization, the choice remains clear: innovate or stagnate. And it's the innovators who shape the future, leaving a lasting legacy of progress and positive change in their wake.

In conclusion, the ongoing journey of innovation is an invitation to embrace change, evolve, and make a mark in a dynamic world. The choice to innovate or stagnate is a defining one, with profound implications for individuals and organizations alike. By choosing innovation, we not only secure our relevance but also play an active role in shaping a brighter and more exciting future.